his first Noel

A Christmas Play

by Joshua L. McKinney

randall house

www.RandallHouse.com

"His First Noel"
By Joshua L. McKinney
Published by Randall House Publications
114 Bush Road / PO Box 17306
Nashville, Tennessee 37217

© Copyright 2007
Joshua L. McKinney

Additional copies of this play may be purchased at www.RandallHouse.com or by calling 1-800-877-7030.

Printed in the United States of America

10- digit ISBN 0892655887
13-digit ISBN 9780892655885

His First Noel

By Joshua L. McKinney

Characters:

Jim—unsaved, dying man / focal point of play
Carol—wife of Jim
Ashley—Jim and Carol's oldest daughter (approximate age 16-18)
Beth—Jim and Carol's youngest daughter (approximate age 7-9)
June—Carol's mother
Sandy—Carol's younger sister
Jamie—Ashley's best friend
Mr. Fields—Carol's pastor
Amos (Buddy)—angel
Kari—angel
Extra angels—number may vary
Jesus—clothed in heavenly garb

> **DIRECTOR'S TIP:** When casting Beth, it may be best to choose an older child (8-10 years old). Although Beth's ideal age is 6, her role is demanding and may be too much for a smaller child. An older child can memorize lines, but dress and act younger in age.

Purpose:

"His First Noel" is very moving and prompts people to analyze their own spiritual conditions, even in the midst of family traditions and holidays. "His First Noel" is a quality Christmas play helping audiences understand the Christ of Christmas, the brevity of life, and the significance of our eternal destiny.

Scene 1

Props:
>Small couch
>Small table and chairs
>Laundry rack or basket
>Assortment of clothes
>Stuffed animal
>Cooking magazines

Setting:
>Center stage should be set as a normal living room with a couch in the middle and a small table and chairs off to the right of the couch. Other props could be added (end tables, rugs, bookcases, etc.) to create a convincing home setting, but these additions are not necessary to the success of the play. Characters should be dressed in casual, modern attire.

DIRECTOR'S TIP: Depending on the amount of space on your stage, you may incorporate Christmas decorations throughout each scene, especially in the living room setting. As the play progresses, you could include more and more Christmas decorations or presents to indicate the approaching holiday. If space and a lack of props are an issue, use painted backdrops to create the setting for each scene. This creates a convincing stage environment and adds to the dynamics of your production.

As the play begins, lights are focused mid-stage. Carol takes clothes off a clothes rack and folds them. Beth enters, carrying her stuffed animal "Buddy." She is followed by June, who is carrying a stack of cooking magazines. Beth continues past Carol and sits on the floor beside the rack while June places magazines on a table and stands behind Carol.

June: We need to look at these magazines, Carol.

Carol sighs and keeps folding clothes.

Carol: Not now, mother.

June: Then when, dear? We need a recipe for the Christmas banquet.

Carol: I'm not going, mom. I've told you that already.

June: Don't be silly. We go every year. The kids love it and everyone at church will be disappointed if you don't prepare something. *She sits and picks up a magazine.* I'll wait until you finish folding those clothes and then we'll look at these cake recipes. How long has it been since we've baked a cake?

Carol finally stops folding clothes and turns to face her mother.

Carol: Mom, you can go if you want. Bake your cake and eat it too. But stop trying to make me go with you.

June: I don't understand you, Carol Ann. You say you want to be more involved in church, that God is moving you into a "closer relationship with Him," but you distance yourself from your friends and skip church functions. Why won't you go to the banquet, dear? Get a little "closer to God!"

DIRECTOR'S TIP: Because Scene 1 presents the family's emotional stress and dysfunction, it is important that characters display exaggerated facial expressions and body language. The dysfunction in the family needs to be portrayed not only through verbal interaction, but also through annoyed and frustrated body language.

Carol looks like she is about to let June have it. But she looks at Beth, who is sitting in the floor playing with Buddy and the anger drains out of her face. She goes back to folding clothes.

3

Carol: I don't want to talk about it right now.

June: Have it your way, Scrooge.

Ashley, Carol's oldest daughter, enters stage right with her best friend Jamie. Jamie sits beside Beth and starts to play with her. Ashley faces her mother from the other side of the clothes rack while Carol continues to fold clothes.

Ashley: Mom? *She drags out this word, as though she wants something.*

Carol: What?

Ashley: Jamie is baking brownies at her house tonight for the Christmas banquet.

Carol: *Glancing at June,* Does she want to bake a cake? *June glares at her.*

Ashley: Her mom's renting a movie.

Carol: I bet mom would enjoy that too!

June: Carol!

Ashley: *Un-phased,* Can I spend the night with her? There's no school; we're out for Christmas. Please?

Carol: No.

Ashley: Why not?

Carol: Because you've got to help me clean the house for our guest.

June puts down her magazine.

June: Didn't you tell Pastor Fields that we wouldn't be taking in a homeless person this year?

Carol: Why would I do that?

June: What do you mean, "Why would I do that?" You know very well why you shouldn't do that! This might be Jim's last Christmas!

Carol: Don't say that in front of Beth!

Ashley: Excuse me? Am I the only person who thinks it's not fair that I have to suffer because you want to take in a homeless person for Christmas?

All ignore her.

June: Maybe I need to say it in front of Beth so you'll begin to realize that it's true! You're acting so strange, Carol. You refuse to spend time with your church family at the Christmas banquet, but you'll happily take a complete stranger into your home.

Ashley: I mean, why do we need to clean up the house for a homeless person, anyway? He might be more comfortable with a full trashcan in plain sight, you know?

Carol: You know what YOU don't understand, mother? You don't understand that all those people at church can do is take my hand and say, "Everything will be alright, honey. We're praying for you." I can't even go to the bathroom without someone quoting scripture to "comfort" me. *Carol uses air quotation marks when she says "comfort."*

June: They love you, Carol. Like I do. Can't you just accept our sympathy?

Carol: You're not giving me sympathy, mother! You're forcing me to keep it on my mind! My husband is dying! Thank you, I know! I change his diapers every day, don't I?

June is shocked. Ashley decides that she better give up and motions to Jamie. Together with Beth, the girls begin to exit stage right.

Carol: Where are you going?

Ashley: I was going upstairs.

Carol: You need to go to the kitchen and sweep and mop the floor. Take Beth with you. I'm sorry, Jamie, but you will need to go home.

Jamie: Yes ma'am.

Jamie exits quickly stage left. Ashley watches her friend go.

Ashley: Why do you act like that?! If you don't want me to go to Jamie's house, fine, whatever. But you don't have to blow up in front of her! You're so embarrassing.

Carol: What did you say to me?

Ashley: Nothing. Never mind. *She turns to exit.*

Carol: Hold it right there, young lady!

June: Carol!

Carol: Stay out of this, June! *June puts her hand to her mouth, shocked at being referred to as June by her daughter.* I am your mother. I will act however I wish in my house. Furthermore, you will show me respect by keeping your comments to yourself. Do you understand me?

Sandy enters stage left. Sandy is Carol's younger sister, who has come in for the holidays but also to help Carol with Jim. She steps on stage and watches the scene unfold.

Ashley: You think you're the only one losing dad, don't you? You're so selfish! You probably won't invite anyone else to the funeral, will you?

Carol stands.

Carol: I told you to keep your comments to yourself. You can believe whatever you want to believe. Now get out of my sight. Go clean the kitchen!

Ashley and Beth exit stage right.

Sandy: What's going on?

June: The usual. Carol is distancing herself from her mother and her daughter. By my calendar, that would mean it's almost

Christmas. Let's get the homeless person in here and make it a real party.

Carol turns to her mother.

Carol: Would YOU like to be homeless, mother? It can be arranged. Just keep running your mouth.

Sandy: Don't talk to mom like that, Carol.

Carol: Or what, Sandy? I didn't ask you to come down here. If it were up to me, you'd be back in Oklahoma.

Sandy: Carol, it's Christmas!

Carol steps forward and delivers her next line directly to the audience.

Carol: Yeah, that's what everybody keeps telling me! Too bad we'll probably be having a funeral. Santa will just have to settle for lilies instead of cookies this year!

June and Sandy stare at Carol, horrified. Suddenly, they hear a voice from backstage.

Jim: CAROL!!!

Carol drops her head and again the anger drains out of her face. Sandy and June are wide-eyed and motionless.

Jim: I BETTER NOT HEAR ONE MORE RAISED VOICE COMING OUT OF THAT LIVING ROOM, DO YOU UNDERSTAND ME? I'M TRYING TO SLEEP!

Carol puts her hand to her brow and walks back to the clothes rack.

Jim: CAROL!? ARE YOU LISTENING?!

Carol: *Shouting,* Y-yes, Jim. *She begins to fold clothes again.*

June reluctantly begins to flip through a magazine. Sandy steps up behind her sister. There's an uncomfortable moment of silence.

Sandy: Maybe you should let your pastor visit Jim, Carol. What do you think?

Carol: He won't have it, Sandy. He never went to church when he was healthy. Why would he want to have anything to do with Jesus on his deathbed?

Sandy: Oh, right. *She turns and looks around, looking somewhat confused.*

Carol: *Not looking at June or Sandy as she says—* Sandy, will you help Ashley clean the kitchen? Mom, will you vacuum? I'll clean the bathrooms. Pastor Fields will be here soon with our guest.

Sandy: Sure, Carol. Sure.

Carol continues to fold clothes, making eye contact with no one. Sandy exits stage right. June stands, takes a few timid steps toward her daughter, then turns and picks up her magazines and exits stage right. Carol is left alone on stage.

Up to this point, Carol has said all of her lines stoically, without any trace of emotion save anger. However, by herself, Carol finally begins to let down her defenses. She stops folding, tries to start again but fails, drops her head and begins to cry. She steps away from the clothes rack, looks around, and runs her hands through her hair. She sits, hesitates, and then puts her face in her hands. She begins to sob. The lights go out.

Scene 2

Props:
Small couch
Small table and chairs
Laundry rack or basket
Assortment of clothes

Setting:
There is no break or change in setting between Scenes 1 and 2.

When the lights go out, Amos and Kari come on stage. As the lights, preferably spotlights, come back on, Carol is still on stage, face in hands, frozen in time. Amos and Kari are standing beside her, regarding her solemnly. Amos and Kari are angels robed in white garments but with otherwise human features.

Amos: Would you look at that, Kari? Have you ever seen anything so sad?

Kari: Probably, but I won't argue with you about it. Why do you ask?

Amos: *Looking shocked,* Do you have a heart, Kari? Did you see what just happened?

Kari: Yes, Amos, I saw what just happened. Indeed, it was very sad. But what can we do about it? And no, I don't have a heart. I'm an angel, not a human.

Amos: You know what I mean, Kari! Don't you feel pity for these humans? It's almost the anniversary of the Lamb's birth and the woman's husband is dying.

Kari: Of course I feel pity for them, Amos. I feel pity for all those we observe, tangled in the sin-curse of the human world. But what can we do? We can't keep the man from dying. It is appointed once for all men to die.

Amos: Hold on, Kari. We should look at this problem "analytically" before we decide that we can be of no aid.

Kari: *Rolling her eyes,* You need to stop watching the humans' television.

Amos: You can learn a lot of things from detective dramas, Kari. Although I'd suggest a sit-com for you. You're much too serious.

Kari: And you're not serious enough! Come now, we need to get going. There might be someone we can actually help elsewhere.

Amos: I'm not going anywhere until we examine this problem! Now, are you going to listen or should I sit down and catch up on *I Love Lucy*?

Kari: *Groans loudly.* Proceed.

Amos: Thank you. Now what do you see here?

Kari: A fool.

Amos: Ha-ha. Are you sure you haven't been watching sitcoms while I'm not looking?

Kari:	Would you be quiet about the humans' television? I see a family, Amos, is that what you want to hear?
Amos:	Correct! What we have here is a family! Do you see any problems with this family?
Kari:	Of course, I do. For one thing, the grandmother is narrow-minded. She refuses to look at Carol's side of the problem and Carol resents her for it.
Amos:	Good observation. What do you think about Ashley?
Kari:	She's confused. Her father is dying and she might be too young to deal with that.
Amos:	Death is something all of the humans must learn to deal with. Don't you think Carol should help her cope? What about Sandy?
Kari:	She's out of her element. She wants to help Carol but she doesn't know how. She's probably just in the way.
Amos:	There you are Kari! Surely you see the common thread in all of these problems!
Kari:	What?
Amos:	*Looking shocked,* Carol! Carol is the heart of this family. All of the other's problems are putting immense pressure on her. Carol needs to make Sandy feel like she's helping out. Carol needs to help Ashley cope with

her father's coming death. Carol needs to make June see her side of the picture. If we can help Carol, then we will help the whole family. The whole situation will be fixed!

Kari: Why are you so blind, Amos! The family isn't Carol's problem—Carol's problem is her husband!

Amos: Well, he is dying, Kari. To her it is terrible, but it is the way of all those under the sin-curse. She can deal with his death. We've helped others like her before!

Kari: No, Amos, we have not. Do you remember what Carol said to Sandy just before Sandy left?

Amos: Carol said a lot of things.

Kari: *Shaking her head,* Listen.

Kari gestures toward Carol, who is still frozen on the stage. The spotlight focuses on her and she raises her head.

Carol: He won't have it, Sandy. He never went to church when he was healthy. Why would he want to have anything to do with Jesus on his deathbed?

Carol returns to her prior position as the spotlight refocuses on Amos and Kari. Amos turns away from Kari, visibly shaken.

Kari: It's not that he is dying, Amos. He's dying without the Lamb. He's dying unredeemed.

Amos:	There must be something we can do.
Kari:	There is not. We are angels. We can never understand redemption, not having suffered from the sin-curse. We cannot lead that man to God. If he dies, he dies as a sinner—not a saint. Carol knows this.
Amos:	There is only one destination for unredeemed man.
Kari:	That is true. Now come, Amos. Let us leave this place of sadness. Let God's will be accomplished.

Kari begins to exit. Amos remains, deliberating.

Amos:	It is God's will that all men should come to Him.
Kari:	*Turns to face Amos,* But it is man's way. We do not know it.
Amos:	What about Beth?
Kari:	What about her?
Amos:	She doesn't understand now, but she will grow up. What will Carol say to her when Beth asks where her father is? Will she tell her that he's in heaven, waiting for her to meet him someday? It will be a lie.
Kari:	*Frustrated,* Amos.
Amos:	No, Kari. They need help. Her husband won't see the pastor and everyone else in

the family is too stricken with their own problems to tell him about Jesus. I don't understand salvation myself, but I must try to show him.

Kari: You'll fail.

Amos: I can't fail until I try . . . with or without your help.

Amos exits, stage right. Kari remains on stage a moment longer. She looks at Carol.

Kari: Then let us try.

Lights out.

Scene 3

Props:
    Small couch
    Small table and chairs
    Stuffed animal
    Cooking magazines
    Watch
    Fake snow

Setting:
Scene 3 is set in the living room as well. Be sure to have enough seating space for all the characters. The clothes and laundry rack should be removed.

To open Scene 3, the lights come on to reveal June, Carol, Sandy, Ashley, and Beth in the living room. June is reading her magazines with Sandy beside her; Carol is looking at her watch; and Beth is sitting in Ashley's lap. They are talking and playing. Beth is playing with her stuffed animal and singing, "My Buddy, My Buddy!" loudly. After the song, Pastor Fields enters stage left.

Carol: Hello, Pastor Fields!

Pastor Fields is decked out in warm clothing and covered in snow. Kari enters behind him, but no one can see her.

Pastor Fields: Hello everyone. *They all acknowledge him.* How's Jim?

Carol: He's . . . he is still with us, pastor. How's the church?

Fields: We're fine. We're praying for you—all of you.

Carol: Thank you, we appreciate your thought-fulness.

No one in the family seems to know what to do next. There is a moment of awkward silence. Finally, Sandy speaks up.

Sandy: How's the weather out there, pastor?

Fields: Terrible! The snow is coming down in sheets! *He looks around, confused by the ackwardness.* Oh! That reminds me!

He quickly exits the way he came in. A moment later, he returns. Behind him is Amos, covered is snow as well and dressed shoddily in human clothes. There are smudges on his face, and his hair is unkempt. When Kari sees him, she puts her hand to her head.

DIRECTOR'S TIP: When casting Amos/Buddy, choose someone who has a good sense of comic relief and timing as well as someone able to build a good rapport with the audience. Amos' character is the comic relief in the play; he begins to lessen the tension as he speaks with each character.

Kari: *She hesitates,* You are crazy!

Amos, although no one can see or hear Kari but him, shoots a menacing glance at her. Everyone stands to meet Amos.

Fields: Everyone, this is . . . *an odd look comes across his face.* That's funny—I don't remember your name . . . In fact, I don't remember picking you up . . . .

Carol: Are you all right, pastor?

Fields: Yes, I'm fine. Um . . . what was your name again?

June: *Eyeing Amos warily,* Yes, do tell us your name.

Amos: *He smiles.* Amos.

Kari, who has been watching this play out, slaps her hand to her face. June looks puzzled.

June: What did you say?

Amos: Um . . .

Kari: Don't tell them your angelic name!

Amos: Uh . . . hey miss! *He steps up and grabs Carol's hand, shaking it furiously. He looks at Beth who is still playing with her stuffed animal like she is the only person in the entire world.* Call me . . . *He hesitates . . .* Buddy.

Carol, who was looking confused up to this point, finally smiles while Buddy continues to shake her hand.

June: "Buddy" what?

Buddy looks at June and smiles sheepishly, then looks around the room. He notices Pastor Fields, who is still shaking the snow off his clothes. He looks back at June.

Buddy: Snow. Call me Buddy Snow.

Kari shakes her head. Carol manages to pull her hand away from Buddy. She gestures toward everyone in the room.

Carol: I'm Carol. This is my mother, June, and my daughters Ashley and Beth. This is my sister, Sandy.

Buddy: It's nice to meet you.

Everyone returns the comment.

Fields: Well, now that everyone is introduced, I better be on my way. There are more guests who need to be taken to their Christmas homes. God bless you. Call me if you need anything.

Everyone gives his or her goodbyes. Pastor Fields exits, stage left.

Carol: Well, Buddy, take off your coat and sit down. Let us get to know you.

Buddy takes off his coat. They both sit down and everyone turns their attention to Buddy. Kari looks both nervous and terribly impatient.

Sandy: So, Buddy, tell us about yourself.

Buddy grins, but otherwise stays quiet.

Kari: Say something, Amos! Stop acting like you've never done this before!

Buddy: *He shoots a glare at Kari,* Well, what would you like to know?

Ashley: Why are you homeless?

June: Ashley!

Buddy: Um . . .

Kari laughs out loud.

Carol:	Ashley Renee Wilson! Don't be so rude. I'm sorry Buddy, you don't have to answer that.
Buddy:	It's ok, Mrs. Wilson . . .
Carol:	Carol.
Buddy:	Carol, I don't mind. I'm homeless because I had to give up my job, Ashley.
Kari:	What! You can't lie, Amos! About anything!
Ashley:	What did you do?
Buddy:	I . . . *looks at Kari* . . . was in security.
June:	*She raises her eyebrows.* Really?

Buddy nods.

Sandy:	You were a security guard?
Buddy:	Something like that.

Kari slaps her hand to her face and shakes her head again.

Ashley:	Why did you give up your job?
Buddy:	Someone needed my help, and becoming homeless seemed like the only way to help.
Ashley:	How does THAT work?
Carol:	I think Buddy's probably said all he wants to say on that subject, Ashley. Whatever the reason, we're glad to have you in our home.

Buddy grins again. Kari shakes her head.

Kari: You got lucky right there, Amos. But you're making a mistake! How can we get you out of this mess!

Buddy looks at Kari and "shhhh's." Beth looks at him funny.

Beth: What's he doing, mommy?

Carol: I don't know, honey. Are you okay, Buddy?

Buddy realizes what he has done and looks panicked for a moment. Yet he quickly recovers, and produces a very loud an animated sneeze, which begins and ends with an exaggerated "shhhh." Everyone looks at him with a puzzled look.

Sandy: Are you sick, Buddy?

Buddy: *Still recovering from his "sneeze."* Oh, no. I'm fine, Sandy. It's just been a while since I've been in someone's home. I could be . . . um . . . allergic to something.

Kari: Don't lie, Amos!

Buddy: *Looks at Kari,* Well I could be!!!

Everyone looks at Buddy again, looking even more puzzled. Buddy smiles and sneezes again.

Buddy: I could be.

Kari: Absolutely crazy!

Carol looks at the others. There is a moment of silence and an exchange of, "I think he's crazy" looks. Carol shrugs her shoulders and finally breaks the silence.

Carol:	Well, I guess I should introduce you to Jim. Then I'll take you to your room and show you where the bathroom is.
June:	*She stands,* It was a . . . pleasure to meet you, Mr. Snow. I'm sure we'll have more time to talk later. Right now, I think I need to take a nap. *She exits, stage right.*
Carol:	All right, Buddy, follow me. *She exits, stage right.*

Buddy stands and follows. As he passes Ashley and Beth, Ashley speaks up.

Ashley:	Nice to meet you, Buddy.
Buddy:	Nice to meet you, Ashley. Hey, by the way, did you empty the trash? To tell you the truth, I'd rather you left it full.

Ashley looks shocked for a moment. She looks at Sandy, who just shrugs.

Buddy:	*Laughing,* I'm just kidding. Folks shouldn't joke about being homeless. It's not that funny to the one actually digging through the dumpster. *He exits. Stage right.*
Ashley:	Did . . . did he know I said that?
Sandy:	I don't know, Ashley. Something tells me we're in for a Christmas like we've never had before.

Kari steps to center stage.

Kari:	You can say that again.

Lights out.

Scene 4

Props:
    Small couch
    Small table and chairs
    Hospital bed
    Medical equipment (IV, monitors)
    Blankets

Setting:

    While the main stage remains untouched, this scene reveals Jim in his bedroom. The bedroom scene can be set off to the left of the main living room setting. Jim is in the hospital bed (or twin bed, creatively set to resemble a sterile, medical environment). Either use real IV equipment or medical monitors hooked up to Jim or simulate with fake props. Jim should be propped up and wrapped tightly in blankets. Use make-up to make his skin pale and eyes sunken. As with the living room setting, you can add chairs, pictures, medicine bottles, etc. to make the room more convincing. Since Carol mentioned changing Jim's diapers earlier in the play, a case of adult diapers set to the side might be an interesting effect.

DIRECTOR'S TIP: To emphasize Jim's illness, use make-up to age and sicken his appearance. Here are some ideas you can use:
1. Use a pancake foundation two or three tones lighter than the skin color/tone of the person wearing it
2. Use a base that has very subtle tints of yellow and green
3. Shadow cheek rouge to make cheekbones more prominent (but not too prominent or zombie-like)
4. Shadow pigment around the eyes, blended subtly and getting darker when closer to the eyes to make them look sunken
5. No lipstick (or at least a very neutral lip rouge)

    Lights on reveal the main stage and the second stage, Jim's room. Jim is in his bed, a hospital bed that has been brought into the Wilson home. There is an IV drip, along with other monitors and other instruments. Jim is asleep. Carol and Buddy leave the main stage area and walk towards Jim's room. Carol looks a bit nervous.

Carol: This room belongs to Jim, my husband. You probably won't be going in here during your stay, but I think Jim wants to meet you. *She starts into the room but hesitates and turns back to Buddy.* Jim is . . . very sick.

Buddy nods. Carol turns back to the room and steps in Jim's room. Buddy follows. The light, which had illuminated the second stage, brightens as the two enter the room. Jim's features are more easily distinguished due to the extra light and he looks terrible. His skin is pale; his eyes are sunken with dark circles around them. He is wearing pajamas; he doesn't awake when they enter the room. Buddy stops at the side of the bed, but Carol continues to the head. Gently, she places her hand on his.

DIRECTOR'S TIP: Although Jim is asleep, he needs to be snoozing propped up on pillows or actually in a recliner chair. If he is laying flat on his back, it will be hard for the audience to hear him or see his facial expressions during this scene.

Carol: Jim, wake up dear. There's someone I want you to meet.

Jim opens his eyes. He looks first at Buddy, then at Carol.

Jim: Who is that?

Carol: This is Buddy Snow. He is our guest for Christmas this year.

Buddy: It's nice to meet you, sir.

Jim: Why is he in my room?

Carol: *Somewhat taken aback,* Well, I just thought you'd want to meet the man who's staying in your home.

Jim: Oh, thank you Carol. You've made my day. *He grabs Buddy's hand and shakes it furiously.* It is truly a pleasure to meet you, Mr. Snow.

Buddy: Oh, Mr. Wilson! Call me Buddy, please.

Jim is being sarcastic. Carol's face flashes anger.

Jim: Well, Mr. Snow—oops, I mean "Buddy"— my friends call me "Sarcastic Sam." YOU can consider yourself a friend.

Buddy: Sarcastic Sam? Really?

Jim: NO! Wow, Carol, where DID the good Pastor Fields find this one? He's dumber than a truck full of bricks!

Carol: I'm sorry, Buddy. Maybe this was a bad idea.

Buddy: Am I still your friend, Mr. Wilson?

Jim: Let me tell you something, Buddy. I don't want you here. My wife might be into the church stuff, but I am not. I think you deserve to be on the streets for Christmas. You're homeless because you don't have a job. You don't have a job because you're dirty and you smell bad. And you're dirty and you smell bad because you're worthless.

Carol: Jim, that's enough.

Jim: No, I'm not finished. Maybe Carol told you that I was sick, Buddy. She was being too kind. I'm dying. I'll probably die before Christmas. So why don't you ask yourself why you're here? I remember telling Carol that I didn't want her to have some Christmas hobo in our house this year. But she "felt like God wanted her to take care of someone." It's not like I need someone to take care of me, right? I guess I see what her priorities are. Don't you wish you had a wife just like her?

Carol is crying. She tries to fight it but fails.

Carol: Come on, Buddy. I'm sorry. *She exits, wanting Buddy to follow, but he stays.*

Buddy: Um, Mr. Wilson, I'm sorry to hear you're so sick . . .

Jim: Oh, you're sorry to hear I'm so sick! That makes me feel a lot better, doesn't it?

Buddy: . . . but maybe you should talk to Pastor Fields. Perhaps he could help you.

Jim: Help me how? Will he help me find Jesus? No thank you. Jesus has never done anything for me, except make my life harder. Ever since Carol "found Jesus" she's tormented me with stupid homeless people every Christmas! She's tortured me with socials and gatherings every Sunday, by getting that fool Fields to call me, and by filling my kids' heads with ignorant

Christian propaganda. And look at me now—lying in bed and dying in my own home. I can't even use the bathroom on my own! Death's almost a reward really, considering all this "Jesus" has done for me.

Buddy: But Mr. Wilson! What about heaven? Don't you want to go there?

Jim: Buddy, if Jesus is in heaven, I'd rather go to hell. Now get out of my room.

Buddy: But . . .

Jim: I said leave!!!

Jim is inconsolable. Buddy leaves the room and goes to the living room, center stage, lost in thought. Alone, he begins to pace and talk to himself.

Buddy: That went well, Amos.

Enter Kari.

Kari: At least you're mastering their humor.

Buddy turns toward Kari.

Buddy: What do you mean?

Kari: Sarcasm, Amos. You're mastering the humans' jokes. Which is good, since you're incapable of helping them.

Buddy: I appreciate your confidence in me.

Kari: See, that's what I'm talking about. Really, you should put on a show before the congregation.

Buddy: He wouldn't listen to me, Kari. When I said the name of the Lamb, he became angry and closed himself off to me. He doesn't even care about his place in eternity!

Kari: These humans do not yet realize the role they'll play in the events to come. Even the ones who serve the Lamb do not fully understand their part.

Buddy: But he won't even listen, Kari! What can I do if he won't even listen?

Kari: Tell me, what would you say if he did choose to listen?

Buddy: I . . . I would . . .

Kari: How would you answer his questions?

Buddy: Well, I'd . . .

Kari: Would you tell him that all men have sinned—all the while being an angel, pure and sinless?

Buddy: Stop it.

Kari: Would you lay out for him the plan of redemption—without understanding what it is to be redeemed?

Buddy: Someone has to!

Kari: Would you show him how to pray—even though prayer is not a privilege of yours? End this foolishness before you do more harm than good.

Buddy: That's enough, Kari. You're right; I am insufficiently prepared for what I face. But so is Jim Wilson. He will die—soon—and right now his soul hangs in the balance. Will we watch? Will we speak soft words to his children and his wife at his funeral, knowing where he is and how he suffers?

Kari: Amos . . .

Buddy: Be silent, Kari! You've spoken and now I will speak. I cannot stand by and watch this family be torn apart. You're right, I don't know the way to the Lamb. But I am a creation of God and I will carry out His will. *He pauses.* And it is God's will that Jim should know Him. Now will you help me, friend, or will you continue mocking me?

Kari waits for a moment, considering Buddy's words.

Kari: I still think this is a mistake . . .

Buddy: Oh, come on Kari!

Kari: . . . but I will trust your judgment in this matter. Yes, I will help you, brother.

Buddy: Thank you, Kari! I knew you had a heart!

Buddy grabs Kari and hugs her. Kari is disgusted and somewhat panicked.

Kari: Why are you hugging me? Angels don't hug! There's no angel hugging in heaven!

Buddy continues to hug Kari despite her protests. Lights go out and Kari quietly exits. Lights come on as Sandy enters stage right. Amos is still "hugging" with no Kari there. Sandy is confused by what Buddy is doing, since Kari has disappeared. Beth is with her.

Sandy: What are you doing, Buddy?

Buddy "lets go" and turns to Sandy, grinning sheepishly. Sandy looks at him with curiosity.

Sandy: Are you . . . okay?

Buddy: Ok? Oh, yeah, I'm great! I was just practicing my hugs!

Sandy: Practicing your hugs?

Buddy: Yeah! I don't get to give many, and, being in a family's home at Christmas, I might need to give a few. I just wanted to . . . um . . . make sure I wasn't rusty.

Sandy: All right (*She says this slowly, as though she doesn't understand, but she still accepts it*). Say, do you know what's wrong with Carol? She ran past me a minute ago crying and locked herself in her room.

Buddy: I think she and Mr. Wilson had a fight.

Sandy:	About what?
Buddy:	*Chuckles.* About me.
Sandy:	Oh, Buddy, I'm sorry. You've got to remember that Jim is very sick. It's a lot of stress for everyone. We're really happy you're here.
Buddy:	I know. You're from Oklahoma, right?
Sandy:	Um, yes I am. How did you know that?
Buddy:	I think I heard Carol say you were.
Sandy:	Oh. Why do you ask?
Buddy:	Oklahoma is a long way from here. I don't understand why you're staying with Carol if you have a home hundreds of miles away.
Sandy:	It's Christmas, Buddy. It's the best time of the year for families to get together.
Buddy:	Yeah, I understand that. But don't you have kids of your own? Aren't they back in Oklahoma? Couldn't a phone call do so you wouldn't need to leave them? Maybe a Christmas card too?
Sandy:	I guess you're right, Buddy. The truth is, I'm here for Carol and mom. In case Jim dies, you know? I want to help them, but . . . *She trails off.*
Buddy:	What?

Sandy:	Never mind. It's nothing.
Buddy:	No, it's okay Sandy. What do you mean?
Sandy:	I . . . I just feel like all I do is get in the way.
Buddy:	I'm sure that's not true.
Sandy:	No, Buddy, you don't understand. Earlier today, Carol told me that she wished I would go back to Oklahoma!
Buddy:	You said it yourself, Sandy. Mr. Wilson is very sick. It's putting a lot of stress on everyone.
Sandy:	I know, but things have never been great between Carol and me, and when dad died it seemed like Carol thought she had to be the new leader of the family. She makes all the decisions herself, even the tough ones. I try to help her out: I clean the house, baby-sit the kids, cook dinner; but I've been here a month and it seems like I'm just getting further away from her instead of getting closer.

Kari enters.

Buddy:	Don't pay any attention to your feelings, Sandy. You're much more appreciated than you know. Sometimes the people we love push us away, although all we want to do is help them. And sometimes those we love don't understand how much we need their help. *He looks at Kari.* But we must

33

continue to love them . . . no matter how hard that becomes. There will be a time when this family needs you and only you and because you love them, you'll be there. That will be worth all the pain you've felt.

A moment of silence passes as Sandy considers what Buddy has said. Her head is bowed, and Beth looks up at her curiously, not understanding what is going on, but content to be where she is. Finally, Sandy nods and looks up.

Sandy: You're right, Buddy. The situation is bad right now, but that doesn't change the fact that we're still family. I'll keep going—and I'll stay strong—for Carol. And Ashley and Beth.

Buddy smiles. Sandy appears to be on the verge of tears when she suddenly remembers something.

Sandy: Oh! No one's shown you your room yet, have they? *Buddy shakes his head.* Wait right here. I'll see if Carol finished cleaning it. If she did, we'll let you settle in and get a bit more comfortable!

Sandy hurries off stage right. She forgets about Beth, whom she leaves standing on stage with Buddy. Buddy looks at her for a moment. She stares back at him.

Buddy: Hi.

Beth narrows her eyes at him. She's grinning.

Beth: I know who you are.

Buddy: Really? Who am I?

Beth: You're an angel!

Kari: Smart kid.

Buddy: And how do you know that?

Beth: Because you want to help my mommy and daddy. Mrs. Powell told me in Sunday School that all angels want to help people.

Kari: What are you going to do now, Amos?

Buddy thinks for a moment.

Buddy: Come here, Beth.

Buddy goes to one knee to be at Beth's height. Beth smiles, waiting anxiously to hear what Buddy is about to say.

Buddy: You're right. I am an angel. But you've got to keep it a secret, okay?

Beth: Why?

Buddy: Because that's the only way I can help your mommy and daddy. Will you keep it a secret for me?

Beth considers it.

Beth: Okay!

Buddy: Ok! *He stands up.* You go find your mommy. I think she needs you right now.

Beth spreads out her arms.

Buddy:	What?
Beth:	Practice!
Buddy:	Huh? *He looks at Beth confused.*
Kari:	She wants a hug!
Buddy:	Oh! Ok! *He bends down and gives Beth a reluctant hug. Kari shakes her head.*

After the hug, Beth runs to the edge of the stage. Buddy speaks up before she gets there.

Buddy:	Beth! *She stops and turns.*
Buddy:	*Puts finger to mouth,* Shhhh.

Beth nods her head and exits. Buddy smiles and shakes his head. He turns his attention back to Kari.

Buddy:	Well, lay it on me.
Kari:	What do you mean?
Buddy:	I told that little girl I was an angel. That's got to be against some kind of rule.
Kari:	I told you that I was going to help you from this point on. That means I'm going to trust your judgment. Right now you need support from me, not reminders of your remarkable incompetence.
Buddy:	Thanks, I think.
Sandy:	*From back stage,* Buddy! Your room is ready!

Kari: You better hurry. You've got a lot of work to do.

Buddy: No, Kari. WE'VE got a lot of work to do.

Buddy hurries off stage right. Kari remains on stage a moment longer, considering what Buddy has said. Finally, she nods her head and follows. Lights out.

Scene 5

Props:
Small couch
Small table and chairs
Cooking magazines

Setting:

The play returns to the main setting—the living room.

The lights come on and reveal June, sitting in the Wilson's living room reading a magazine. Buddy enters, stage right. He's cleaner, and sporting a new set of clothes. He looks lost in thought. He stops near center stage and turns toward the audience. He doesn't notice June, but she notices him.

June: Good morning, Mr. Snow. Did you sleep well?

Buddy: I don't really sleep much. How about you?

June: About as well as can be expected. I'm up half the night nowadays. I see you found a new suit of clothes.

Buddy: Yes, Sandy brought them by my room last night.

June: Those are Jim's clothes from years ago. He doesn't have any use for them now. I heard you met him last night.

Buddy: That didn't go too well.

June:	I'm sure you understand why. I feel for you, Mr. Snow, I really do. I can't imagine living on the streets. But Jim is sick—sick unto death, mind you—and he doesn't understand why Carol would bring a stranger into his home at the twilight of his life. Honestly, I don't understand either.
Buddy:	*Sits down on the couch,* Don't you think she has a kind heart?
June:	It has nothing to do with her kind heart, Mr. Snow! Jim and Carol love each other very much . . . or they did, once. After Ashley was born, Carol began attending church and, praise God, gave her life to the Lord Jesus. After that, a rift formed between them.
Buddy:	What do you mean?
June:	It has to do with Jesus and sin. When we are born, we are born with a sinful disposition. This causes us to do wrong; when we die we cannot enter into heaven because God cannot be in the presence of our sin. However, if we accept Christ as our Savior—and I hope you have, Mr. Snow—then our sins are covered by Him and we receive a second nature—a godly one.
Buddy:	Interesting.

June:	Very. Yet, our old nature does not go away and we still have the ability to sin. We are always in conflict with our first nature, until we die and go to heaven where there is no sin.
Buddy:	Yes, that is true, there is no sin in heaven.
June:	You speak as though you've been there!
Buddy:	Well, yes I have . . . I mean . . . I have in . . . my mind! When I close my eyes I can see the "pearly gates"!
June:	I'm glad to hear you're a believer.
Buddy:	Oh, I believe, all right. But what does this have to do with the rift between Carol and Mr. Wilson?
June:	Like I said, the godly nature conflicts with the sinful one. While Carol has two natures, Jim, regretfully, has only one. Jim can't understand why Carol is so devoted to God and Carol can't understand why Jim doesn't want to know Jesus.
Buddy:	I see.
June:	After Beth was born . . . SHE was a surprise to all of us, let me tell you . . . we found out Jim was sick. Since then, things have gotten worse; Jim and Carol can't even have a civil conversation. Now we find ourselves here, with you in our home.
Buddy:	What do you think needs to be done?

June:	Carol needs to realize how bad off Jim is. She trounces around here doing chores and yelling at Ashley like everything is fine, while her husband lies in his bed struggling to breathe.
Buddy:	Have you tried helping her?
June:	That's easy to say but hard to do. Carol doesn't WANT my help. She won't accept comfort and she won't accept sympathy. She . . . *June pauses, and seems to be lost in thought and on the verge of tears . . .* I lost my husband many years ago. I know how painful it can be, especially if it takes you by surprise. Carol has what I never had—a chance to say goodbye to her husband, a chance to prepare for the sadness that will hit once he's gone. How do I make her understand that?
Buddy:	*Stands up and goes to June's side,* Have you tried just being her mom?
June:	*Shocked,* What do you mean? Of course I have! I'm always her mother!
Buddy:	Maybe you shouldn't act like you have all the answers, June. Maybe that's not what Carol needs. Don't be the tough veteran who's "been there before." Don't think you can solve your daughter's problems by baking cakes with her or making her listen to people who keep reminding her that her husband is dying.

June: How did you . . . ? *She lets it go.* If that's not what a mother is, Mr. Snow, then what should I be?

Buddy: Just be her mom.

June looks up at Buddy with tears in her eyes. Realization is washing over her face, and she finally understands what Buddy is saying.

Buddy: She does need you, June. But she needs you to love her, not guide her. She needs to know you're there for her . . . that you support her, whatever she does. She needs to comfort her daughters and you need to comfort her.

Buddy stands, smiles, and exits stage right, leaving June by herself on stage. Slowly, she rises.

June: *Still teary-eyed,* That man . . . that man is an angel. *She exits, stage right. Lights out.*

Scene 6

Props:
Small couch
Small table and chairs
Plate of cookies

Setting:
The setting remains the same with a few additions. The table and chairs are the focal area of this scene. Place a large plate or jar of cookies on the table.

> **DIRECTOR'S TIP:** Place a small bookshelf behind the table stocked with small kitchen appliances and other pantry goods. The extra props will bring the focus to the table area for this scene.

Lights come on to reveal the living room later in the same day as Scene 5. Beth enters, stage left, running, smiling and looking for a hiding place. She finds one under the table. Ashley and Jamie then enter, stage left.

Jamie: Hmmmm. I wonder where Beth went? *She's kidding.*

Ashley: I don't know, Jamie. *Beth giggles loudly.* Maybe we should look around.

They pretend to search for Beth, looking under chairs and appliances and anything else on stage. While they're looking, Buddy enters stage left and is visibly confused at what they are doing. He begins to search around his area; Ashley and Jamie do not realize he is there.

Finally, Ashley and Jamie come to the table. Ashley is the closest and points to where Beth is hiding. Jamie nods her head and Ashley silently counts down from three. When she reaches three, they both look under the table and make funny "Gotcha" sounds. Beth laughs hysterically as they pull her out from under the table.

Buddy watches all of this. He jumps when the girls scream and scratches his head when they pull Beth out from under the table. They all begin to laugh. Still confused, Buddy steps forward.

Buddy: Boogity-boogity-boo!!! *This is loud, accompanied by hand gestures and an ugly face.*

The girls, not knowing Buddy was there until that moment, scream. Buddy screams in return.

Ashley: Buddy! What are you doing?

Buddy: *Shaken,* What are you doing?

Jamie: We were playing a game with Beth!

Buddy: Oh! Of course! A game! *He pauses.* Boogity-boogity-boo!!!

The girls, not expecting this, jump and scream again.

Ashley: Stop it, Buddy! We're not playing anymore!

Buddy: Sorry.

Jamie: *Laughs,* It's all right . . . just let us know that you're behind us next time, okay?

Buddy: *Gives a thumbs-up,* Gotcha.

The girls reluctantly return the thumbs-up, laughing because no one really does that anymore. They stand on stage for a moment, no one sure what to do next. The silence becomes awkward.

Buddy: Soooooo . . . Can I play the game too? I mean, when you start again?

Jamie:	I don't know. It was a spur-of-the-moment kind of thing.
Ashley:	Yeah, we were just coming in here to get a couple of cookies.

Beth, still on the floor from the game, jumps to her feet and runs to Ashley. She pulls on her clothes as she speaks.

Beth:	Please, Ashley? I'm not hungry anymore. Let's play the game with Buddy! *She turns to Buddy and gives him a thumbs-up.*
Ashley:	No Beth. Besides, I bet Buddy is hungry too.
Buddy:	No, I don't eat. Let's play the game!

Ashley gives Buddy a strange look, then, not understanding the comment, looks at Jamie. Jamie shrugs her shoulders.

Ashley:	*Sighs,* All right. We'll close our eyes and count to ten.

Ashley and Jamie put their hands over their eyes and begin to count. Beth, giggling, runs back under the table. At "four" Buddy realizes he is supposed to cover his eyes too.

Ashley:	Ok, here we come. Where's Beth? *She looks at Jamie beginning to "search" for her.*
Jamie:	I don't know, Ashley. Where IS Beth? Beth!!!
Ashley:	Beth!!!
Ashley & Jamie:	BETH!!!

Buddy looks at the girls, then he looks at Beth under the table, and then he looks back at the girls. He points to Beth.

Buddy: She's right there.

Ashley: Buddy! Look for her!

Buddy: I did. She's right there. Does that mean I win?

Jamie: You found her too soon.

Buddy: Do I get a prize?

Ashley: Nobody "wins' the game, Buddy. That's not why we play.

Buddy considers this for a moment. He shakes his head.

Buddy: I don't know about this. . . . I think you guys are just mad because I beat you so fast. It's just a game. We can play again.

Beth: *Runs out from under the table,* Yeah! Let's play again!

The girls make gestures signaling their surrender considering the subject. Carol enters, stage left. She is wearing a coat, and has just come in from town.

Carol: Hello girls. Hello Buddy. How are you _today?

Buddy: I'm great! I just won the game.

Carol: Oh yeah? What were we playing?

Buddy: I'm not sure what it's called, but between you and me your daughter's not too good at it. And she's a sore loser.

Carol: *She laughs,* I could have told you that. She gets it from my side. Are you hungry?

Beth: I am mommy!

Ashley: *Reaching for the cookies,* We were about to get some cookies. You want one?

Carol looks at Ashley strangely, and walks to the table. When she gets there, she searches for something but doesn't find it.

Buddy: You know how to play too!

Carol: *Ignoring Buddy,* Ashley, where is the chicken I bought last week?

Ashley: In the freezer, I guess.

Carol: What did I ask you to do this morning?

Ashley: You . . . uh-oh.

Carol: Yeah, "uh-oh." What did I ask you to do?

Ashley: You asked me to set out the chicken so it would be thawed by the time you got home. I'm sorry.

Carol: Yes, you are. I just don't understand what world you're living in.

Ashley: What world? What are you talking about?

Carol: Be quiet! You know exactly what I'm talking about. What have you done all day? Have you even started any of your chores?

Ashley: I did all my chores yester . . .

Carol: I told you to be quiet! You have chores every day, young lady. Being out of school doesn't give you the right to do nothing. You and I are going to have a long talk. *She looks at Jamie and Beth.* Go to your room, Beth. Go home, Jamie.

Jamie: Yes ma'am!

Jamie exits stage left, Beth stage left. June, who was on her way into the room entering stage right, stops. June stands on the far right of the stage and watches what transpires in the following exchange. No one notices her, except Buddy, of course.

Anger washes onto Ashley's face.

Ashley: I can't believe you! I said I was sorry! Can't you just accept my apology?

Carol: You need to learn responsibility, Ashley. One mistake here, another mistake there. They add up. I'm not going to be here forever. I can't take care of you for the rest of your life.

Ashley: You don't take care of me now! You make my life miserable!

Carol: Is that so? In two more years you can test that theory if you want. You can do what you want, and make your life whatever you feel like making it. Just don't come begging to me when you can't feed and clothe yourself . . . when you're freezing and you don't have any warm place to sleep. *She pauses.* But that won't happen, will it? You'll stay here for at least five more years because you never learned responsibility!

Ashley: How can you say that? Don't you love me at all?

Carol: *Shocked,* How dare you say such a thing. How dare you. You know what? I think I've figured out what your problem is. I love you too much. I was too easy on you when you were younger. I spoiled you.

Ashley: Oh yeah, Mom. That's it.

Carol: And disrespectful too. Oh well. You reap what you sow, I guess. Go to your room. I don't want to see you the rest of the night. I'll send Sandy up later with a sandwich.

Ashley starts to storm off stage right. As she goes, she says "I hate you," under her breath.

Carol: What did you say?

Ashley: *She stops,* Nothing.

Carol: No! You said something, little girl. Let's hear it. Let's hear how mature you are.

Ashley: Just forget it, Mom.

Carol: I'll decide what I wish to forget! Now tell me what you said!

Ashley: I . . . I . . . I said . . .

Ashley clenches her fists, hesitates, and then lets Carol have it.

Ashley: I said I hate you! I said I would give anything I had to be somewhere else, away from you! You make me hate living! And you know what else I said? Every night I ask God why—why it's not you in that bed. Why it's not you dying!

Ashley runs off stage leaving Carol and Buddy near center stage and June at the far right. Throughout the exchange, June has reacted appropriately to what was being said. Buddy looks uncomfortable and Carol looks shocked.

Carol: Could you give me a moment, Buddy?

Buddy nods and exits stage left. Carol sits down at the table, laying her head in her arms. June approaches and puts her hand on her daughter's shoulder.

June: Are you all right, dear?

Carol: *She raises her head,* I don't know what else to do, mother. She's so angry. I think she really does hate me.

June: She doesn't hate you.

Carol: Yes she does! She wishes I was dead!

June: She was just angry. She didn't know what she was saying.

Carol:	I'm the one who doesn't know what she's saying, mother. I stood here, in this very room, and told my daughter that I wanted her to leave . . . that if she was hungry or cold not to come back because I wouldn't help her. What's worse? That I'm saying it or that I know what I'm saying and I can't stop? She should hate me; I hate myself. She is what I've made her. It's my fault.
June:	Carol Ann, you are an excellent mother.
Carol:	Yeah, right!
June:	You really are. You are what I raised YOU to be. I taught you how to be independent, how to take care of yourself, how to be a strong woman. I taught you how to be a good wife and a good mother. And this is what you've taught Ashley. However, there were times in your life when you didn't need a mother; you needed a mom. And that's something I never taught you to be. Yet that's where Ashley is right now. She doesn't need someone to tell her to do her chores or to ground her. Her father is dying without Jesus, and she doesn't understand why. She needs her mom.

Carol is crying by this point. Throughout the conversation, she has set at the table with her hands on her face. But when June finishes, Carol turns to take her hand. June bats Carol's hand away and embraces her daughter. Carol is still sitting, so it looks as though Carol is shorter than June. This symbolizes the nature of their relationship after June's revelation— even though Carol is all grown up, June is still her mom.

June: *Still embracing Carol,* First, dear, you need to pray. Pray that God will give you peace, and pray that God will touch Ashley so she'll realize that she didn't mean what she said. When this happens, she'll come to you. That's when you can show her you love her. That's when you can be her mom.

June kisses Carol on the top of her head and begins to exit stage left. Carol stops her.

Carol: Mom . . .

June: Yes, dear?

Carol: I love you.

June smiles, and tears well up in her eyes.

June: I never forgot. *She exits stage left.*

Lights out.

Scene 7

Props:
Bed
Blankets and pillow
Nightstand
Lattice covered in ivy
Two full backpacks
Tambourines

Setting:
The stage will be completely transformed for this scene. Center stage is now a bedroom—the guest room for Sandy. The lights should be darkened to insinuate night. On stage two, previously Jim's bedroom, is the ivy-covered lattice to indicate the outside of the house.

> **DIRECTOR'S TIP:** If your stage is large enough, set up the outdoor scene and Sandy's bedroom stage right. Sandy's bedroom could be on stage, while the outdoor scene could be just in front of the stage. This will save time and keep you from removing the living room props. If your stage is too small for this idea, interject a small intermission at this point in the play to provide ample time for the stage transformation.

As the lights dimly shine, Sandy's room is revealed. She is sound asleep in the bed. Buddy is standing in front of the lattice, looking up at the stars. Kari enters the scene after a moment and steps beside Buddy. She begins to stare too.

Buddy: The universe is big, isn't it?

Kari: Yes, it is.

Buddy: Have you ever flown to any of them. You know, the stars?

Kari: Yes, I have. They're beautiful.

Buddy: *He points,* That one . . . right there. That one's my favorite.

Kari: I didn't care much for that one. *She stares for a moment, then points.* That one . . . do you see it? That star has a planet, a massive ball of gas with this intense red color, as red as any of the rubies in heaven.

Buddy: Wow. *He pauses a minute, thinking.* You know, I think He made them like that. None of these stars are half as beautiful as the sights in heaven. Yet each one has a piece of heaven shining through.

They stare a bit longer.

Kari: How are things going in there? *She points toward the house.*

Buddy: Well, kind of half and half. I think I've helped June and Sandy, but Jim still won't let me in his room. Carol won't talk about anything other than the weather, and every time I start to talk to Ashley she gets in trouble.

Kari: You're doing everything you can, Amos.

Buddy: It's not enough. Jim doesn't have much time.

Kari: You can't overcome death.

Buddy: I know but . . .

The lattice behind the two shakes.

Buddy: Did you hear that?

Kari: What was it?

The lattice rattles again. Buddy and Kari turn around and look at the lattice. It shakes again. They get close to the lattice and look up.

Kari: Isn't that Ashley?

Buddy: Angels in heaven, it is!

Kari: What's she doing climbing out of her window? The sun has been set for quite a while.

Buddy: She and Carol had a terrible argument. She must be running away.

Kari: That's not good.

Buddy: That's an understatement. Listen, I need your help.

Kari: Why? Shouldn't you just get her mother?

Buddy: No! I've got to talk Ashley out of running away without her getting into more trouble.

Kari: Why do you need me?

Buddy: Ashley's room is next to Sandy's. We might make some noise when we're talking and that might wake up her aunt. If that happens, Ashley will be in, uh, what the humans call "hot water."

Kari: How am I supposed to keep her asleep?

The lattice shakes. Buddy looks at it worrisomely.

Buddy: I don't know . . . sing to her! I've heard stories of humans falling asleep because they heard the soft singing of a beautiful angelic voice.

Kari: Ha! Not this angelic voice! I didn't make the heavenly chorus, remember?

Buddy: Kari!

Kari: I don't even know any songs!

The lattice rattles.

Buddy: Yes you do! Our last assignment was with that youth choir, remember? We helped those kids memorize the words to their songs.

Kari: Sure, but I don't think any of those songs could . . .

Lattice rattles, louder than any time before.

Buddy: Just go, Kari! You said you were going to trust my judgment! *He pushes her toward Sandy's bedroom. She starts walking that way.*

Kari enters Sandy's room and the lights on the outdoor scene go out temporarily. Kari stands beside Sandy's bed and looks at her unsure.

Kari: I think I'll just try talking to you. *Sandy lets out a loud snore/moan and turns over in her bed. Lights on center stage go out as lights on the outdoor scene come on.*

The lattice shakes and Buddy is holding a backpack looking up. He waits on Ashley. Moments later, Ashley steps out from behind the lattice and onto stage two. She is dressed warmly and carrying another backpack. She doesn't notice Buddy, keeping her back to the audience while she dusts herself off.

Buddy: Hey Ashley! Whatcha doin?

Startled, Ashley turns quickly.

Ashley: Buddy! What are you doing out here?

Buddy: I was looking at the stars. They're beautiful tonight, aren't they? What are you doing?

Ashley: I . . . um . . . the same thing.

Buddy: Really? Why didn't you just use the front door instead of climbing out of your window?

Ashley: Well, I needed the exercise.

Buddy: Right. You know, there's a word that people use . . . usually it implies that someone is cold, but in other instances it means that someone or something is . . . okay . . . all right . . . good.

Ashley: Cool?

Buddy: Yes, that's the word! Cool! *He looks at the stars.* That's what I am. I'm cool. Cool, as in, if you're not really out here looking at stars, you can tell me. I'm not going to get your mom.

Ashley looks unsure for a moment.

Ashley: Okay, you got me. I'm not looking at stars.

Buddy: What's going on?

Ashley: Well . . .

The lights on center stage come up as the lights on the outdoor scene go down. Kari is bent over Sandy's bed. She's speaking softly and deliberately.

Kari: You are very relaxed. You are very content. You are dreaming happily. You are in no danger of waking up . . . *Sandy stirs, and makes a loud snore. Kari looks worried.*

The lights go out on stage one as the lights come up on the outdoor scene.

Ashley: I'm leaving. You heard what mom said earlier. She wants me gone. So I'm going— two years early.

Buddy: That's not what she meant.

Ashley: Then what DID she mean? When your mom looks at you and says she won't feed you when you're hungry or take you in when you're freezing to death, I think it's time to go.

Buddy: Your mom loves you very much, Ashley. There's a lot going on that you don't understand.

Ashley: I understand. I understand she's selfish. She's not the only one losing someone— Beth and I are losing our dad.

Buddy: *Frustrated,* Tomorrow is Christmas Eve. Where do you think you're going to go?

Ashley: *Defensive,* There's a shelter downtown. I'm going to stay there tonight, then hitch a ride out of town in the morning.

Buddy: You shouldn't run from your problems.

Ashley: I'm not running! I'm . . . escaping them. They're clamping down on me. I'm just getting out before the trap is set.

Buddy: Life is full of traps. Do you think you can escape every one of them?

Ashley: I'm not strong enough, okay, Buddy? Not right now! Mom expects me to do so much. And Beth . . . she looks up to me. When dad's gone, she'll want to know why. And what am I going to tell her? I don't know why either!

Buddy: You don't need to understand the why. You just need to be strong. That's what Beth will remember . . . that you were there for her.

Ashley: Oh, sure, that sounds good. Did you get it off a Hallmark card?

Buddy: A what?

The lights go out on the outdoor scene as the lights come up on stage one. Sandy is tossing and turning.

Kari:　　　　This isn't working! "Sing to her!" That's easy for him to say. He's not the one up here, is he? And he's not helping by talking so loudly. *Sandy makes a loud sound, but this time like she's talking in her sleep.* What am I going to do? She'll be awake any minute.

Kari thinks for a moment wondering what to do. Then, after looking around sheepishly, she stands up. She looks very uncomfortable. She clears her throat.

Kari:　　　　*Singing,* Swing low . . . *pause* . . . sweet chariot . . . *pause* . . . Coming for to carry me home.

She looks at Sandy to see if it's working.

Kari:　　　　*Singing,* Swing low, sweet chariot. Coming for to carry me home.

She begins to sing the first verse, looking and sounding more comfortable as she goes along. She even begins to sway a little. She closes her eyes and goes into a slow spin. She doesn't notice Sandy sitting up, looking around, and then getting out of bed. Kari: *Singing,* I looked over Jordan, and what did I see? Coming for to carry me home, A band of angels coming after me. Coming for to carry me home. . . .

The lights go out on stage one as they come up on the outdoor scene.

Ashley: A Hallmark card! A sympathy card. That's a nice line, but a little unrealistic, don't you think?

Buddy: No, not at all. Everyone has a choice. How your family recovers from this, how you recover from this, is ultimately in your own hands. You've got more living to do, Ashley! Don't mess up your life now, before it even gets started.

Ashley: You're just like mom. You want me to be strong, to plaster a smile on my face and keep on going, like nothing is wrong. I've been strong for three years and I can't be strong any longer. I wish . . . *She trails off.*

Buddy: You wish what?

Ashley: I wish . . . I wish someone would be strong for me.

Sandy: I will.

Buddy and Ashley turn. Sandy has entered stage left and is staring at Ashley intensely.

Buddy: Sandy! I thought you were asleep!

Sandy: I was . . . but someone, I guess you two, woke me up. To tell you the truth, I thought someone was talking to me.

Buddy: *Under his breath,* Kari!

The lights on stage two go out as the lights on stage one come up. Kari is really into it now, singing as loudly as she can and raising her hands to the sky. There are two other angels with her, swaying in sync and playing tambourines.

DIRECTOR'S TIP: When the lights come back on Kari and company singing "Swing Low, Sweet Chariot," it would be humorous for a full angelic choir to be on stage with music playing and everyone singing the chorus. If you do not have enough choir members, cueing music at that time would still show Kari's progression into musical bliss.]

Kari: IF YOU GET THERE BEFORE I DO, COMING FOR TO CARRY ME HOME. *She looks around and notices that Sandy is gone. She halts her swaying and singing but the angels keep going.*

Kari: Uh-oh.

The lights on stage one go out as the lights on the outdoor scene come up.

Sandy: I'm glad I came out here though. What's going on?

Ashley: I'm . . . I'm leaving.

Sandy: Why? That's not going to fix anything.

Ashley: Then what do you want me to do? I can't stay here, living this way! I'm not strong enough!

Sandy: Didn't you hear me? I said I would be strong for you.

Ashley: Aunt Sandy, I . . . *On the verge of tears.*

Sandy: Shhhh. Come here.

Ashley and Sandy embrace. Ashley begins to sob, and Sandy gently strokes her hair.

Sandy: Why do you really want to run away?

Ashley: *Still crying,* Because of mom. She's killing me; I need her so much.

Sandy: Then why don't you tell her that?

Ashley: She won't let me!

Sandy: Nonsense. Go to her, right now. She'll listen. She doesn't have a choice.

Ashley: She's pushed me away before. What will make this time any different?

Sandy: Because, you're her daughter. Deep down inside her, whether she knows it or not, she needs you as much as you need her.

Ashley tries to speak but can't. She manages a weak nod.

Sandy: Come on. Let's go back inside. I'll walk you up to Carol's room.

They begin to exit, stage left, Ashley in the lead. Sandy turns back to Buddy before she leaves.

Sandy: Thank you, Buddy.

Buddy nods and Sandy and Ashley exit. They pass Kari rushing to join Buddy on stage.

Kari: Oh, Amos! I tried, really I did. I even sang!

Buddy: It's okay, Kari. Everything turned out fine.

Kari:	Truthfully?
Buddy:	Of course! You know we can't lie. Sandy found her chance to help the family; Ashley decided not to run away; I spoke with June earlier; and I think that in a few moments, Carol will be much happier as well.
Kari:	That leaves Jim.
Buddy:	Yes. *He looks toward the stars.* That leaves Jim.

Lights out.

Scene 8

Props:
Small couch
Small table and chairs
Stuffed animal
Hospital bed
Medical equipment
Recliner chair
Stool

Setting:
The main stage switches back to the regular living room setting. Off to the left is Jim's bedroom complete with hospital bed and items used in Scene 4. A recliner needs to be added to the room.

Lights come on to reveal the Wilson's living room. Carol, Beth, and Ashley are sitting and talking. There's a difference in Carol and Ashley's attitude toward one another. Beth is playing with her stuffed animal, Buddy.

Ashley: Are you sure you don't want to go? You could use a break.

Carol: I'm sure. I need to stay with your dad. You can go with Sandy and your grandma. Sandy needs to get out of the house anyways.

Ashley: What about you, Beth? Do you want to go to the Christmas banquet?

Beth shakes her head, almost comically. She holds up Buddy, like that should be answer enough.

Ashley: *Laughs,* All right. I'll bring you some cookies. How's that sound?

Beth nods this time, smiling widely.

Sandy, June, and Buddy enter stage right.

June: Are you ready Ashley?

Ashley: Yep! I'm glad we're getting there early to help set up. It will feel good to actually be doing something productive since school let out.

Sandy: Hey, there's nothing wrong with being lazy every once in a while.

June: Hush your mouth, Sandy Claire! I raised you to know better than that. What did I always say?

Sandy, Carol, and Ashley look at one another.

Sandy, Carol, and Ashley: Laziness may appear attractive, but work gives satisfaction.

June: That's correct. And as you can see, Mr. Snow, all of my girls are happy.

Buddy: You raised them well.

Ashley: What about you, Buddy? Are you going to the banquet?

Buddy: No, but I appreciate the offer. You go and have fun.

Sandy: We will have fun. Lots. Isn't that right, ladies?

June and Ashley give their affirmatives. Ashley stands, goes to Carol and hugs her. The three women exit, stage left. Buddy, Beth, and Carol are left on stage.

Buddy: I'm glad to see that you and Ashley worked out your problems.

Carol: I am too. We had grown apart over the last few years. It was time we got back on track.

Kari enters, stage left.

Buddy: You have a wonderful family, Carol.

Carol: I'm blessed beyond what I deserve, Buddy. Sometimes I just need to remind myself of that.

Buddy: Still, you worry about Mr. Wilson.

Carol: Jim and I have grown apart too. I'm afraid it's a little too late for us.

Buddy: It's never too late.

Carol: *She forces a smile.* Our problems don't arise from lack of love. There's only one Person who can help Jim now, and Jim doesn't want to have anything to do with Him.

There is a moment of silence. Even Beth feels the awkwardness in the room. Finally, Carol stands.

Carol: I should go sit with him. It is Christmas Eve. Come on, Beth. *Carol and Beth exit,* *stage right. Beth leaves her stuffed animal. Buddy stands after they leave.*

Kari: What now?

Buddy: I'm not sure. That man needs the Lamb, but he won't let me tell him what I know and Carol has all but given up.

Kari: You'll think of something, Amos.

As Buddy and Kari stand on stage brainstorming, Beth enters, stage right. She picks up her stuffed animal, then stands beside Buddy, looking at him expectedly.

Buddy: Whatcha doin', Beth?

She holds up Buddy, again, as though that is answer enough.

Buddy nods, and goes back to brainstorming. Beth waits another moment.

Beth: What are you doing?

Buddy: I'm thinking.

Beth: About how to help daddy?

Buddy: Yes. He's very sick.

Beth: I know. He's sick right here. *She points to her heart. Buddy nods.*

Beth: Tell me about Christmas, Buddy.

Buddy looks at her a little strangely, then he looks at Kari. She shrugs her shoulders.

Kari:	There's no harm in it.
Buddy:	Ok. *He sits down in one of the chairs.* What would you like to know?
Beth:	Everything that's important.
Buddy:	*He laughs,* All right. Well, a long time ago, there was a man and a woman. His name was Joseph. Her name was Mary. One day, God sent an angel to Mary to tell her that she was going to have a baby.
Beth:	That was Jesus.
Buddy:	Yes, that's right. His name is Jesus. He is God's only Son. *He stops for a moment, as if gathering his own thoughts.*
Buddy:	Several months after this happened, Joseph had to go on a trip . . . to a town called Bethlehem, where his father was from. He had to take Mary with him, but she was almost ready to have Jesus. When they finally got to Bethlehem, they couldn't find any place to stay the night. Finally, an innkeeper made room for them in a stable, where animals live. That's where Jesus was born.
Kari:	Hey, tell her about the shepherds! That's my favorite part. I'll never forget the looks on their faces.
Buddy:	Near Bethlehem there were shepherds— people who take care of sheep. An angel appeared to these men and told them

about Jesus. After that, a host, or a lot, o:
angels sang praises to God.

Beth: Were you there?

Buddy: Yes, I was there. We were all there. *He
pauses, lost in thought.* After we left, the
shepherds went to the stable and worshiped
Jesus. And that was the first Christmas.

Beth considers what Buddy told her for a moment.

Beth: And Jesus . . . He came to earth to die for
my sins, right?

Buddy: Um, yes. He did. But He didn't stay dead.
He arose three days after being crucified.

Beth: And everyone who believes in Him will
live forever.

Buddy nods.

Beth: Sooo . . . you can't have Christmas without
Jesus.

Buddy: No, not really. Christmas has become a lot
of things since the first one, but really, it's
all about Jesus. It's only about Jesus.

Beth: *She smiles,* Ok! Thanks! *She exits, stage
right.*

Kari: What was that all about?

Buddy: *He stands,* I don't know. She's a little girl—
one of Yahweh's strangest creations.

Kari:	I don't know . . . you're definitely the strangest.
Buddy:	*Laughs,* No more jokes, Kari. We've got to think. Mr. Wilson doesn't have much time left.

The lights on stage one go down as the lights on Jim's bedroom come up. On stage two is the hospital bed with Jim in it. Beside him is Carol asleep in a recliner chair. There's a stool next to the bed.

Beth enters stage left, leaves her stuffed animal next to the stool and climbs into the bed with Jim. He opens his eyes, weakly. He is much sicker than he was in Scene 4.

Jim:	Hello, little bit. What can I do for you?
Beth:	Tomorrow is Christmas, daddy.
Jim:	Yeah. Aren't you glad you've been such a good girl?
Beth:	I'm worried about you, daddy.
Jim:	Oh yeah? Why's that?
Beth:	Because you don't have Jesus. You can't have Christmas without Jesus.
Jim:	*He looks around. He is angry, as angry as he can be in his condition.* Who told you that? I've had plenty of good Christmases without Him.
Beth:	Not this Christmas, daddy. I know you're leaving . . . and I know you're not coming

	back. I want to make sure you have Christmas with Jesus.
Jim:	Be quiet, Beth.
Beth:	Did you know that He died on a cross for my sins, daddy? It was bad. It hurt Him a lot.
Jim:	I know.
Beth:	And then, three days later, He arose. Now He lives forever, and because I believe in Him, I will too.
Jim:	I'm glad you do, baby. But daddy can't believe in Jesus. Daddy has done too many bad things.
Beth:	I've done a lot of bad things too, daddy! Remember when I stole the cookies from the grocery store? Remember when I broke Ashley's music box? Remember when I lied to grandma about cleaning up my room?
Jim:	I've done a lot worse.
Beth:	It doesn't matter! Mrs. Powell said that Jesus died for everyone—that means you too!
Jim:	Beth . . . I don't know how . . .
Beth:	I do! Pray!
Jim:	I don't know how to pray.

Beth: I'll show you! *She bows her head and closes her eyes. She waits a moment, then peeks to see if Jim is doing the same thing.* Come on, daddy!

Jim who is crying by now, hesitates, then bows his head.

Beth: Dear Jesus, thank You for this day, and thank You for Christmas. I have someone who wants to talk to You. *She whispers the next part.* That's you!

Jim: *Hesitates,* Hello God. I . . . I've never prayed to You, mostly because I was afraid. I was afraid You wouldn't take me. I was afraid I had done too much wrong. *He pauses.* I know my life is almost over . . . I'm sorry I waited so long. But . . . will You forgive me? I'm a sinner . . . I need You. Come into what's left of my heart. Save me, Jesus.

Beth: Please remember my mommy and grandma and Ashley and Aunt Sandy. Keep them safe.

Jim: Oh, God! Please take care of my daughters . . . and my wife. Bless them throughout the rest of their lives. Please let them remember that I loved them very much. And keep your hand on them, and help them to always follow You . . . so I can see them again some day.

Beth: Thank You for loving me, Jesus.

Jim: Thank You for loving me, Jesus.

Beth: In Jesus' name we pray, Amen.

Jim: Amen.

Jim and Beth both look up. Beth is smiling, and so is Jim
He's still very sick, yet he looks different. He looks happy and a.
peace. He's smiling.

Beth: Now you can have Christmas, daddy!

Jim: *Definitely crying by now,* Listen, Beth. I
             love you very much. Do you . . . *He pauses.*
             He puts his hand over his heart. . . Do you
             understand that?

Beth nods.

Jim: Good. Never forget it. When mommy
             wakes up, tell her what happened. Tell her
             I'm having Christmas with Jesus. *He rubs*
             his chest.

Beth: Ok! You're going to live forever now,
             daddy!

Jim: That's right, Beth. I'm . . .*he lays his head*
             back and says weakly . . . going to live
             forever. *He smiles.*

Carol wakes up and stands. Thinking Jim is asleep, she tries to
wake him.

Carol: Jim? Jim, honey, wake up. *Beth smiles at*
             her. Oh no . . . oh no . . . please no! *She*
             begins to panic and weep. Not right now!
             Give us more time! *She collapses on Jim,*
             sobbing.

Beth gets out of the bed and looks around, searching for something or someone.

Beth: Buddy? *Carol, grieving ignores her.* Buddy!

Beth runs off stage shouting, "Buddy!" The lights on stage one come up and she runs on stage. She is looking for Amos.

After Beth exits, Carol realizes her daughter has left. Still crying, she tears herself away from Jim, stops to pick up Beth's stuffed animal, and runs after her daughter.

When Carol steps on stage one, the lights on Jim's bedroom go out. She grabs her daughter and kneels down in front of her. She holds out the stuffed animal.

Carol: What are you doing, Beth? Here he is! Here's Buddy! *She offers Beth the animal. Beth throws it on the ground.*

Beth: No, not that Buddy! Buddy Snow! Our guest this Christmas!

Carol: What are you talking about? You know we didn't have a guest stay with us this Christmas. Your father . . . he didn't want us to . . . *she trails off.*

Beth: You don't remember Buddy? *Carol doesn't answer.* He was an angel! He really was an angel!

Carol: Shhh, Beth. I need to tell you something about your daddy.

Beth: No, I need to tell YOU something about daddy. He prayed, while you were asleep, and now he's like us! He's going to live forever!

Carol: What are you talking about?

Beth: It's daddy's first Christmas, mommy. He's got Jesus now!

Carol tries to shake her head, but Beth nods emphatically to rebuke her. Finally, Carol reluctantly nods to her head too. Beth smiles.

Carol: Praise God! Praise God!

She grabs Beth and they embrace. Buddy and Kari enter, Buddy stage left and Kari stage right. Buddy is now dressed like an angel.

Kari: Can you feel it, Amos? The angels are rejoicing in heaven!

Amos: Yes, one who was lost has now been found.

Kari: Praise be to the Lamb! Highest honor and glory be found in His name!

Amos: Praise be unto the Lamb, who takes away the sins of the world.

Musicians begin to play the Christmas carol, "Hark the Herald Angels Sing." The lights on stage dim until total darkness fills the room. All over the auditorium, angels with beautiful robes wonder through the crowd. They carry candles (electric or regular). As they enter they begin singing the first verse of "Hark the Herald Angels Sing" making their way to the stage. As the spotlights begin dimly shining, revealing Amos and Kari kneeling over Carol and Beth, with their hands on their shoulders. They are comforting them. The angelic choir continues singing the first verse, they form an arc around the four characters. When they finish singing the first verse (and possibly the second if it takes that long to get everyone on stage), Amos speaks.

DIRECTOR'S TIP: To keep with the serious tone of the play, sing "Hark the Herald Angels Sing" at a slower tempo than normal. The words of this song fit in well with the theme of the play. A slower tempo will aid in setting the mood for reflection.

Amos: Be blessed, Carol, you and your family as well. I'll never understand redemption, but I know you have been redeemed. Follow God for the rest of your days, and you will see Jim again, but more important, you will see Jesus, the One who gave you eternal life.

The angels begin singing the third verse. They still form an arc, but at its center is Jesus, who has entered from backstage. From the crowd comes Jim, in a robe, on to the stage. He falls at Jesus' feet, but Jesus lifts him up and embraces him. Kari and Amos take their places at the ends of the arc. They look at each other and smile, and the lights go out. Everyone but Jesus exits the stage and lights come on again showing Jesus with his arms stretched out.

Jesus: Will you come to Me?

Lights go out.

The End.

DIRECTOR'S TIP: Due to the nature of this play, you may choose to offer an invitation to receive Christ at the end of this production. Ask your pastor or church leader to explain the gospel at the close of the program. Also, be prepared for a response! Designate people to be praying for non-Christians attending the play. Ask several qualified volunteers to be on hand to minister to anyone who chooses to accept Christ.

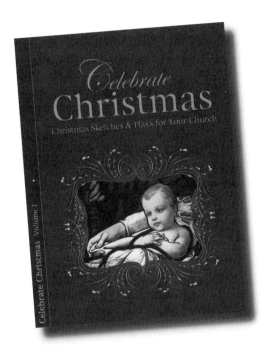

Celebrate Christmas
Various Authors
$19.99
ISBN 0892655860

Celebrate Christmas is a collection of 15 different dramas perfect for the Christmas season. The dramas vary in length, from 10-minute sketches to full-length plays, and will fit the needs of every church, whether large or small.

Heaven Came Down
Jack Dale
$5.99 each or $4.99 each when ordered in
quantities of 35 or more
ISBN 0892655879

This full-length drama is set in the Biblical era
and begins 15 months prior to the birth of Christ.
"Heaven Came Down" portrays events that may
have taken place in heaven and what did transpire
on earth before Christ's birth and uses traditional
hymns to help tell the story.

To order call 1-800-877-7030 or
visit our website at www.RandallHouse.com